Raising Rabbit Handbook for Beginners:

Detailed Guide on How to Effectively & Carefully Raise Rabbit as Pets & For Nutrition Purposes (Meat); Includes Its Care; Feeding; Choosing a Breed; Its Home & So On

By

Markus J. Muench

Copyright@2020

TABLE OF CONTENTS

CHAPTER ONE

INTRODUCTION

Raising Rabbits

Raising bunnies is straightforward and affordable. Two does and one buck should deliver 180 pounds of meat for every year.

Obviously, there are Angoras (with their excellent, white, long hide) and other "extravagant" breeds. In any case, these are not meat bunnies. In common occasions a significant number of the little rabbit raisers try not to spare the skins, however they do have some worth. At the present time, for instance, purchasers are offering from 30 pennies to $1.50 each per pound. You can get names of purchasers from a rabbit/bunny magazine.

Jack began with a "trio" — a youthful buck nine months old and two does of a similar age. He reproduced the does soon after he got them. The next month he had 17 rabbits. Seven is a large enough litter, as indicated by the specialists, for one doe to raise. So Jack annihilated four from one litter of 12 and gave the other doe an extra to bring her litter of six up to seven. Jack scoured a little Mentholatum on her nose so she was unable to smell the distinction between her own and the youthful one from the other litter.

At seven weeks every one of the 14 of the youthful bunnies was alive and playful. At this age they weighed 44 pounds. The two does were reared once more.

The next chapters will explain to you all you need to understand from a to z regarding both the raising of rabbit as pets as well as for meat purposes. Happy perusal!

CHAPTER TWO

THE BENEFITS/GAINS OF RAISING RABBITS AS WELL AS WHAT TO FEED THEM WITH

Jack kept some cautious records.

This is what he gained from them.

A Chinchilla gauging three pounds, live weight will cost you from 25 to 35 pennies or somewhat more to raise. You'd pay a dollar, in any event, in the market for him.

Jack made sense of how much time it took him to raise a three pound fryer. It took one hour level. That is, he clarified, "I invested 14 hours real task energy — as a name amateur — raising 14 meat-suppers for the family. I could slice that down the middle, yet I like puttering around them."

Jack had such good karma with the bunnies that, obviously, I needed to perceive what I could do. Jack, who is a most liberal, disapproved of individual, kept us provided with bunny — he continued saying that after all he needed to pay "lease" in some structure or other for the pen. Myself and a friend both preferred rabbit without question; it tastes something like chicken however has an "immovability" that chicken doesn't have. I get it was a year prior to when I got my pen back and got to keeping bunnies myself.

By chance, after we got the bunnies we wouldn't fret raising them to eat — I surmise in the wake of eating a few rabbits raised by another person it's simpler to go into bunny raising carefully from the stance of raising them for meat and not let yourself make pets of them. Obviously, when you can put rabbits or chicken or whatever else in a cooler and leave them there for half a month or months you'll see that you consider them "meat" — not "adorable creatures."

What to Feed Rabbits

Each rabbit box ought to have a hayrack. This you keep brimming with roughage — the rabbit/bunny specialists suggest Alfalfa, however a decent, verdant clover feed is okay. Timothy isn't as rich in protein as the very clover, however in the event that it's appropriately restored it's superior to an ineffectively relieved clover or Alfalfa. The rabbits can deal with the roughage better on the off chance that it is cut up in three or four inch lengths. (Take a bunch, press it into a pack and saw it off into a crate with a normal hand saw.) You can likewise take care of vetch, dairy animals' peas, and other rich feeds. You can give your rabbits/bunnies dried pieces of bread as well as crusts; likewise any sort of vegetable parings and tops they'll eat. You can take care of them with grass trimmings plus weeds. In any case, don't leave what they neglect to eat in the pen. Take it out following day and quite soon you'll discover what they like best and the amount to take care of them. Rabbits relish carrots and other root vegetables. Feed green nourishments sparingly from the outset if your rabbits aren't utilized to them. Once in a while they eat excessively and swell or get looseness of the bowels.

You additionally feed them one of the readied rabbit pellet nourishments or entire grain — they don't appear to like any grain that is ground up excessively fine. You can ask the man you purchase your bunnies from for bearings with regards to what he's discovered the best techniques for taking care of.

CHAPTER THREE

HOW FREQUENT DO RABBITS UNDERGO MULTIPLICATION?

How Quick or Frequent do Rabbits Multiply?

Everyone has a tale about how

quick rabbits duplicate. I recollect

a companion of mine who had a little family and stressed over this while getting his bunnies. Truth be told, he concluded that he'd start with the base a solitary doe and a solitary buck. He was a sales rep and each time I'd see him I'd ask, "Well, what number of bunnies have you now." The main month it was only two. The second month it was two. The third month it was as yet two. About this time my companion started to stress over his bunnies not duplicating. Furthermore, when, toward the finish of the fourth month, he despite everything had just two, I started to get somewhat dubious. Sufficiently sure, he didn't have a doe and a buck — he had two bucks!

Deciding the sex of a bunny is simple. Get the man you purchase your bunnies from to show you.

I locate that two does and a buck produce 40 or 50 bunnies per year to eat. At three pounds or more that is all our family needs.

You breed about like clockwork. Growth just takes 30 to 32 days. The youthful medical attendant for five or a month and a half, figuring out how to eat as they come. At six or seven weeks you put the youthful fryers in another cubby or two and eat them among at that point and ten or twelve weeks. Or on the other hand you process the entire delicate harvest at eight or nine weeks and fast freeze all aside from the one you need for supper at that point.

You can eat them as fryers until they're seven or eight months old and fully developed. In any case, at that point they've eaten a lot of genuinely extravagant food and in this way aren't such an extensive amount a deal, cost-wise. Better isolated the youthful bucks from the does at a quarter of a year.

You can murder off old rabbits toward the finish of a couple or even three years and make a stew out of them. The skin from a develop bunny is worth impressively more than from "fryers."

CHAPTER FOUR

RAISING RABBITS AS WELL AS NURTURING RABBITTS FOR MEAT AND A SPECIAL RECIPE FOR YOU

Raising and Nurturing Rabbits for Meat

Raising bunnies is probably the least complex thing you can do

right in your estate. In addition to
the fact that they require little
consideration, however they
likewise give a lot of meat.

One of the main undertakings I
needed when we moved to our
place in the nation was bunnies. I
had perused commonly that they
delivered astounding tasting meat
at little expense.

One payday when I happened to
peruse a promotion offering a six
compartment, all-metal wire box
available to be purchased for under
$20 I was unable to oppose this

great purchase. The cubby in the long run came, yet my girlfriend was as yet incredulous and, in any case, we were up to our necks getting our outbuilding wrapped up, figuring out how to drain, running our oven battery, keeping an eye on our honey bees and goats and setting the geese. It wasn't difficult to put off getting the bunnies for some time.

At that point, a companion of mine, a male friend, Jack in particular, saw I hadn't done anything with my rabbit/hare box and he inquired as to whether he

could utilize it until I prepared.
That was okay with me. He
obtained the box, set it up in his
carport and started looking into
the subject of bunnies.

Customary German Hasenpfeffer Recipe

Here is a formula for the renowned
German method of getting ready
bunny. Cut up your bunny meat
and put it into a container. Spread
with vinegar or wine and water,
equivalent parts. Include one cut or

more, onion, salt, peppers, barely any cloves, cove leaves.

Give this splash access a cool spot for two days. At that point evacuate and wipe the meat dry and earthy colour it completely in a griddle, in hot spread, turning it regularly. Bit by bit include the sauce or squeeze you salted it in, and let stew about thirty minutes, until delicate. Prior to serving, mix in one cupful of thick acrid cream. It is set!

CHAPTER FIVE

PICKING THE PERFECT RABBIT BREED PLUS CREATING A RABBIT HUTCH

Picking a Rabbit Breed

Jack picked an assortment called

the Chinchilla. You can take your

pick of a few decent meat breeds.
Jack preferred the medium
measured varieties, which weigh
around eight to 10 pounds
developed. You could go in for the
Flemish Giants, for example, that
occasionally gauge 20 pounds.
They eat significantly more,
obviously, and their fryers, at seven
to nine weeks, weigh not all
substantially more than do those of
the medium varieties at a similar
age. The New Zealand Whites are
another well known medium
weight breed — their white hide is
worth more than the Chinchilla.

There are various other acceptable medium weight breeds.

You can "inbreed" with no damage. Simply keep a youthful doe or two out of a litter and breed her to your equivalent buck when she's around seven to nine months old. You can amaze your reproducing times, having one new litter coming in like clockwork from one doe or the other. Be that as it may, in the event that you embrace this framework, you can't trade the youthful between the does. Each three or four years purchase or exchange for another buck.

And keeping in mind that we're regarding the matter of purchasing, attempt to get great, sound and solid creatures. You couldn't care less about a "show" hare, however get great blood. They may even cost you from $10 to $25 a trio; you aren't probably going to set aside cash by beginning with $3 worth of cleans. Nonetheless, don't stress over family or immaculate markings or blue strip champs.

Creating a Rabbit Hutch

Rabbits/bunnies are exceptionally strong creatures, simple to raise and very spotless. They can stand a ton of chilly climate, yet they can't stand a significant wetting and sweltering climate gets them down. They wear fur garments in summer recollect. They must have clean feed plate and clean water. They need a cool, obscure summer place with loads of ventilation, some daylight sporadically and a decent rooftop. We keep our metal pen in the stable. We clear it out once every week and keep a lot of straw on the floor and in the home box (a nail barrel with a strip across it). In winter, we water the rabbits night and morning, taking the water out before it freezes. In summer we keep the water plate in every case full. They drink a great deal.

CHAPTER SIX

PERFECTS & DEPENDABLE TECHNIQUES TO CARE FOR ONE'S RABBITS; STEP BY STEP GUIDE

The most effective methods to Care for a Pet Rabbit

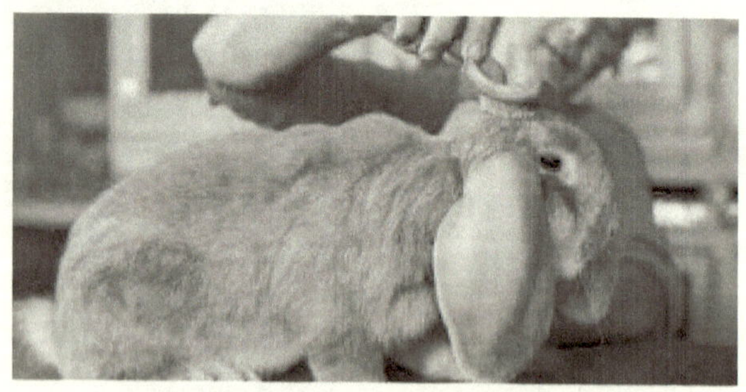

Bunnies are one of a kind pets.
They have explicit requirements so
as to live a long, glad and sound
life. Here is an essential outline on
the most proficient method to
think about a pet bunny:

Stage 1: Set Up Safe Indoor Housing

Hares inside playing. There are a
few choices to house bunnies
inside. They can live free-reign in a
rabbit sealed room/rooms, or they
can be contained inside a pup pen,
rabbit apartment suite, or huge
rabbit/hare confine. Whenever

contained, their space ought to consistently be sufficiently huge so they can bounce around, and they ought to be let out of their pen for in any event a couple of hours regularly for work out.

Ensure the essential area of your hare isn't detached from you and your family. A family room or parlor is a decent spot. Become familiar with indoor bunny lodging at Housing Your Pet Rabbit Indoors.

Stage 2: Bunny Proof Your House

Wire cover rabbits need space to go around and investigate. So as to make a sheltered space for your rabbit and to ensure your assets, you should altogether rabbit evidence the territory. This incorporates covering all wires with plastic sleeves or flex tubing, or lifting them 3-4 feet far from your rabbit/hare.

On the off chance that you don't need your baseboards chewed, you can cover them with plastic gatekeepers, 2x4s or furring strips. You'll likewise need to close off specific zones since bunnies like to bite the undersides of beds, things on shelves, house plants, and that's just the beginning. Essentially, your hare will attempt to bite everything in reach.

Stage 3: Provide Fresh Hay

Rabbits eating hay. A rabbit's eating regimen ought to mostly comprise of feed. New roughage ought to be given to rabbits consistently. Infant rabbits ought to be given horse feed, and grown-

up bunnies ought to be taken care
of with timothy feed, grass feed, or
oat feed.

Utilizing a huge feed feeder is
useful on the grounds that it keeps
a lot of feed dry, clean, and open.
Study the significance of roughage
and where to get it at Hay for

Stage 4: Provide Fresh Greens, Fiber-rich Pellets, and Fresh Water

Rabbits eating greens. Supplement your bunny's roughage with new vegetables, fiber-rich pellets (in constrained amounts for grown-up hares), and new water every day. You can become familiar with what sorts of food to take care of your rabbit at what to feed your pet rabbit.

You can likewise find out about becoming a large number of your hare's preferred vegetables at Bunny Gardening for Beginners.

Stage 5: Set Up a Litter Box

Rabbits in litter boxes. Rabbits have a characteristic tendency to crap and pee in one region. Exploit this by setting up a medium-sized feline litter box or shallow stockpiling canister close to their food/water bowls and roughage feeder.

Put a flimsy layer of rabbit safe, reused paper pellet litter at the base of the litter box. Try not to utilize dirt/clustering feline litter or wood shavings, as they are undependable for hares. At that point put feed on head of the litter. Rabbits like to eat feed and crap simultaneously, so this will energize great litter box propensities.

Stage 6: Provide Enrichment

Bunny in cardboard castle. Rabbits can get exhausted without any problem. In addition to the fact that they need space to work out, they additionally need mental incitement. Cardboard manors are incredible on the grounds that rabbits go through hours biting new windows and entryways. Cardboard palaces additionally give a calm shelter to the rabbits when fundamental.

You can likewise give an assortment of toys to your rabbits to arouse their curiosity. Get some bunny, logic toys for rabbits, and playing with your pet bunny.

Stage 7: Groom Your Rabbit

Rabbit's nails, rabbits are normally spotless creatures and wash themselves habitually. Be that as it may, you despite everything need to prep your bunny all the time. Bunnies experience shedding cycles two or three times each year. It's essential to brush your bunny to expel the entire overabundance hide. Something else, your rabbits could ingest it and have genuine stomach related problems.

Customary nail cutting is likewise significant in light of the fact that long nails can get caught on things or they can twist into your bunny's paw. Figure out how to cut your rabbit's nails yourself by simply clipping your rabbit's nails as expected.

Stage 8: Bring Your Rabbit to a Rabbit-Savvy Vet

Veterinarian with rabbits. Rabbits are prey creatures, thus their characteristic sense is to conceal any side effects of disease. You should keep a careful gaze to guarantee your rabbit is eating, drinking, crapping, and peeing normally. In the event that you notice any adjustment in conduct, it is essential to call a rabbit adroit vet right away.

Notwithstanding reacting to sickness, it is additionally fundamental to get your rabbit for customary veterinary tests. The vet doctor can toughly inspect their body parts to ascertain if they are healthy. At long last, think about fixing or fixing your rabbit. Fixing can decrease forceful conduct, improve litter box propensities, and improve a rabbit's general wellbeing.

Stage 9: Understand Rabbits' Unique Language and Behaviour

Resting rabbit. Pet bunnies are not quite the same as felines and canines. It's basic to see how rabbits think so you and your bunny can carry on with a glad coexistence.

My rabbit hates me; that's your reaction! By taking into account your rabbit's normal tendencies, you can fabricate a trusting, adoring relationship with your rabbit. Happy rabbit raising to you!

THE END

www.ingramcontent.com/pod-product-compliance
Lightning Source LLC
Chambersburg PA
CBHW020941160726
47993CB00007B/2883